★ ★ ★ ★ ★ ★ ★ ★ ★ ★ ★ ★ ★ ★ ★ ★ ★ ★

# BACK-TO-BACK

## Super Bowl Champions Peyton and Eli Manning

★ ★ ★ ★ ★ ★ ★ ★ ★ ★ ★ ★ ★ ★ ★ ★ ★ ★

## An Unauthorized Biography by Hugh Hudson

**PSS!**
PRICE STERN SLOAN

PRICE STERN SLOAN
Published by the Penguin Group
Penguin Group (USA) Inc., 375 Hudson Street, New York, New York 10014, USA
Penguin Group (Canada), 90 Eglinton Avenue East, Suite 700,
Toronto, Ontario M4P 2Y3, Canada
(a division of Pearson Penguin Canada Inc.)
Penguin Books Ltd., 80 Strand, London WC2R 0RL, England
Penguin Group Ireland, 25 St. Stephen's Green, Dublin 2, Ireland
(a division of Penguin Books Ltd.)
Penguin Group (Australia), 250 Camberwell Road, Camberwell, Victoria 3124, Australia
(a division of Pearson Australia Group Pty. Ltd.)
Penguin Books India Pvt. Ltd., 11 Community Centre, Panchsheel Park,
New Delhi—110 017, India
Penguin Group (NZ), 67 Apollo Drive, Rosedale, North Shore 0632, New Zealand
(a division of Pearson New Zealand Ltd.)
Penguin Books (South Africa) (Pty.) Ltd., 24 Sturdee Avenue,
Rosebank, Johannesburg 2196, South Africa

Penguin Books Ltd., Registered Offices:
80 Strand, London WC2R 0RL, England

*Photo credits:* Top cover photo: courtesy of AP Photo/Darron Cummings; bottom cover photo courtesy of AP Photo/Stephan Savoia. Insert photos: first page courtesy of AP Photo/ Mel Evans; second page courtesy of Jed Jacobsohn/Getty Images, Scott Boehm/Getty Images, Ben Liebenberg/Getty Images; third page courtesy of Joe Robbins/Getty Images, Scott Boehm/Getty Images; fourth page courtesy of Jeff Haynes/Getty Images and Gabriel Bouys/Getty Images.

*Library of Congress Cataloging-in-Publication Data is available.*

ISBN 978-0-8431-3354-7          10 9 8 7 6 5 4 3 2 1

# BACK-TO-BACK

## Super Bowl Champions Peyton and Eli Manning

**An Unauthorized Biography by Hugh Hudson**

*PSS!*
PRICE STERN SLOAN

# TABLE OF CONTENTS

★ ★ ★ ★ ★ ★ ★ ★ ★ ★ ★ ★ ★ ★ ★ ★ ★ ★

# INTRODUCTION

Thousands of fans packed into the streets of downtown New York City, surging forward for a better view as Eli Manning held up the Vince Lombardi Super Bowl Trophy for them to see. The cheer that went up was almost deafening. In the city that never sleeps, everything had come to a standstill for one team and one man.

Just the day before, Eli had beaten the odds and led the New York Giants to a last-minute victory over the then-undefeated New England Patriots. The Patriots hadn't lost a single 2007 regular-season game and they were the clear favorites to win the Super Bowl. But in the end, the Giants and Eli stopped them cold. "It's just surreal," Eli said to *Sports Illustrated* after the game in the locker room.

The next day, at the head of the Giants' Super Bowl parade, Eli soaked it all in. The rush from the game had faded, but the glory was still there. It was a bitterly cold and rainy morning in February. But despite all of that, thousands of Giants fans had shown up to cheer on their team. The parade couldn't be stopped. "MVP! MVP!" the crowd cheered again and again. The whole team rolled through the avenues of New York City, finally stopping in front of City Hall. Giants players Plaxico Burress, Brandon Jacobs, and their coach Tom Coughlin were mobbed as well, but Eli Manning was definitely in the spotlight. As he smiled down at all of the fans from the top of the steps, it all finally caught up to him. The Giants had won the Super Bowl. He had done it. Eli signed autographs with his teammates as he made his way to meet the mayor. He wore a mile-wide smile on his face and a championship ring on his finger.

Mayor Michael Bloomberg praised all of the Giants that day for their 17–14 victory over the New England Patriots in Super Bowl XLII, but the *New York Daily News* reported that he had special words for Eli. "On Sunday, he showed the world the heart of a true champion." After that, Eli made his own speech as Super Bowl MVP. "I would not trade any moment for this moment right here," Eli said. "Standing up here in this city, going to the parade, it's been a true honor. Thank you."

It wasn't such a different scene from the one only a year before in Indianapolis. There, the colors were blue and white, the team was the Colts, and the MVP was Peyton Manning. In a year when the Colts were not expected to even make it to the playoffs, Peyton carried his team to their first Super Bowl since 1971, beating the Chicago Bears, 29–17, in Super Bowl XLI. Thousands of fans showed up at the RCA Dome for the Colts victory celebration. Peyton's skill as quarterback had made the win possible. He was the MVP, but Peyton remained humble. "I've never taken for granted what we've had, not for one single game, not one single practice," Peyton would say later to USA Today. "I've truly been blessed."

The Manning brothers had done it. Two brothers. Two back-to-back Super Bowl victories. Two back-to-back Super Bowl MVP awards. There were some who doubted them, but the Manning boys never let their critics get them down. They were always there for each other, no matter how hectic life became. And life for these two brothers from Louisiana was hectic indeed.

# CHAPTER ONE
## Growing Up Manning

Even when they were little, the Manning boys weren't like everyone else. Their father, Archie Manning, was a famous NFL quarterback, and in the Manning household, football meant everything. They saw their father's face every day on billboards and TV. When the season was going well, people would cheer wherever they went, but when the season was going poorly, the Mannings couldn't escape the crowd's displeasure. No matter what was happening, football affected everything in their lives. It was a part of who they were.

Archie Manning grew up in Mississippi. His family didn't have a lot of money, but Archie worked hard in school and eventually won a football scholarship to the University of Mississippi. Also known as Ole Miss, the college was one of the biggest football schools in the south. Archie was extremely motivated, a talented football player, and he was soon leading his team as the Ole Miss starting quarterback.

In 1970, Archie led the Ole Miss Rebels to a Sugar Bowl victory, and he was named as an All-American player while in college. Archie met his future wife, Olivia, while they were both students at Ole Miss. Olivia was very supportive of Archie's dreams to play pro ball. Archie also excelled at baseball, and the Atlanta Braves tried to draft him after college. But Archie's true love was football, and he turned the Braves down to register for the NFL Draft.

The New Orleans Saints drafted Archie in 1971 to be their starting quarterback. The Saints were a relatively new team to the NFL and they didn't have a very good record, but they thought for sure that a talented new quarterback like Archie could turn their luck around.

The Mannings had always been a tight-knit family, and Archie was sad to leave them behind in Mississippi. Luckily, Archie wouldn't be alone in New Orleans. He married his college sweetheart,

Olivia, and the couple bought a beautiful house in the historic Garden District of New Orleans. Archie was ready to make a name for himself as a quarterback, a husband, and as a father! Archie and Olivia's first son, Cooper, was born in 1974. Two years later, little Peyton Manning was born on March 24, 1976.

Peyton weighed twelve pounds at birth and by the time he was two years old, he was already busting out of his clothes and getting into his parents' hair. Peyton may have been a bundle of energy, but he was also a good kid and was very respectful of his parents.

Peyton learned his good manners from watching his father. "I got to watch my dad as a kid, how he handled himself after games with fans, with the media. I can remember, as a kid, just how patient he was, and how courteous he was to his fans," Peyton said, years later, to the *Academy of Achievement*. It really made an impression on Peyton that, even though his father was famous, Archie never let himself get too big to spend time with his fans.

Still, growing up the son of a famous football

player wasn't always easy.

Archie was a loving father, but playing for the Saints meant that he wasn't home very often. Between practices, games, public appearances, charity work, endorsements, and travel on the road, Archie was a very busy man. Many times, Peyton would have to wait until Sunday to see his father—and that was when Archie was on the field during a game! But whenever Archie was home, he always made time for his sons. "Don't ever get too proud or too old to say that you love me and to say that you love each other," Archie would say, according to the *Academy of Achievement*, scooping up his boys into his arms. Cooper and Peyton really looked up to Archie, and they were supportive no matter how their father did on the field.

The fans in the Superdome weren't always as kind. Over seventy thousand people would cram into it to watch the Saints play every week, and they made their presence known. They would throw things at the players and shout out cruel names when the games didn't go well. Even though Archie led the NFL in completions and yards for a quarterback in only his second season, he was still the target for a lot of angry fans. During his time with the team, the Saints never had a winning season and the fans were quick to blame the quarterback. But Archie wasn't the problem—the team just couldn't come together. In fact, Archie was named NFL MVP in 1978, and made the Pro Bowl in 1978 and 1979. He was playing well—it just wasn't enough.

Whenever Peyton went to see a game, he had to hear the crowd boo when Archie made a mistake or was blamed for a bad play. But that was the life of an NFL quarterback, and Archie never complained. He was playing professionally, after all, and that was what he had always wanted to do.

Peyton caught the football bug early on from his dad and older brother. He loved the sport, but when he was little he never thought he'd end up following in his father's footsteps. "I certainly didn't think at five, six, seven years old that I would be doing that same profession," Peyton told the *Academy of Achievement*. He couldn't get enough of the game, though. He would stay up all night, listening to broadcasts of games on the radio, and he followed the Saints and Ole Miss's progress every season.

Even though Peyton didn't think he would go pro, he liked playing football as much as he liked watching it. No one took these little games seriously, but Archie and Cooper went out of their way to play with Peyton and make him feel like he was part of the "team." Some of Peyton's favorite childhood memories are those spontaneous games when he got the chance to bond with his father and brother. "I feel very fortunate to have the kind of support I had as a child," Peyton said to the *Academy of Achievement*. Peyton and his older brother were very close and Peyton really looked up to Cooper. Cooper was only a couple of years older than Peyton, so they developed a friendly rivalry during those backyard games. That rivalry only intensified when Cooper went to grade school and began to play on his first football team.

"My personality was very different from my dad's," Cooper said to the *Associated Press*. Cooper loved his little brother, but that didn't mean he always went easy on Peyton. Cooper would occasionally use his little brother as a practice dummy, and he was quick to tease gullible Peyton.

When sibling rivalry threatened to cause a rift between the boys, their mother was always there to step in. She was a constant source of love and support for her sons. Together, the family was happy, healthy, and flourishing in New Orleans, but things couldn't stay that way forever.

1980 was a difficult year for the Mannings. The Saints had once again missed the playoffs and the stress was getting to Archie. Many fans were blaming the Saints' losses on Archie, despite his excellent performance. The Saints just couldn't catch a break, and by the end of that season the Manning family knew that changes were in the works. Archie's contract was about to expire and he had to decide what to do. The Saints were unlikely to re-sign him, but Archie didn't want to uproot his family. If he went to a different team and his family stayed in Louisiana, though, he would see them even less than he already did.

Peyton was only five, but he still remembers that tough time. "When everybody knows who you are, you could be more easily embarrassed because more people are looking at you," Peyton said. Little did the family know then that the possibility of moving was just the first of many changes in store for them.

# CHAPTER TWO
## Another Manning in the Mix

Amidst all of the tension with Archie's career, there was one bright spot for the Mannings. On January 3, 1981, their third son, Elisha Nelson Manning, was born. Peyton must have been thrilled about the arrival of Eli—it meant he was no longer the littlest brother!

That year was the last that Archie would play for the Saints. The next season, Archie became the starting quarterback for the Houston Oilers. Rather than force his family to move, Olivia convinced Archie to keep the family in New Orleans while he played in Houston. Archie was only a few years away from retirement, so it didn't make sense to move the family. Staying in New Orleans meant that Cooper, Peyton, and Eli could continue their happy childhoods at home.

With Archie out of the house, Olivia really took

charge of the family. She frequently took the boys to see their grandparents in Drew, Mississippi, or to her own family in Philadelphia. Houston wasn't too far away, so Archie still got to visit often, and the Mannings continued to be a tight-knit family. Archie credits his wife with how smoothly that time period went, calling her "The Great Equalizer." "She can take a crisis and get it right back to normal because she's very levelheaded," Archie said to the *Associated Press*. "She doesn't holler and scream, she just handles it. It's a great trait."

Having well-behaved kids did help. As Olivia later said to *CBS Sportsline*, "They were good kids. We never had any trouble with them." And Eli was the most well-behaved of the bunch. He was always the quietest brother, but Olivia and Archie weren't worried about him. He was calm and patient and very mature for such a young age. Plus, as he got a little older, he was more than able to stick up for himself when Peyton and Cooper teased him too much. The boys played baseball, football, and basketball together, and playing sports could sometimes bring out the competitive edge in all the brothers.

When playing HORSE, "Anybody that got even close to scoring would get a forearm to the nose," Cooper said to WLTV in Louisiana. "It would end up with Dad coming out and breaking up the fight." Despite the sibling rivalry, the Manning brothers were actually pretty close. They relied on one another for support and did their best to keep one another out of trouble. As soon as he was big enough, Eli joined his big brothers in their pickup football games. "A bunch of his friends would come over and he'd [Peyton] make me be permanent center," Eli said to AOL Sports. Eli was a solid and steady player, allowing Peyton and Cooper to pretend to be superstars. They even sang the national anthem before their pickup games. "We were very, very official," Peyton said, laughing, in an interview with IGN.com. As the brothers got older, football became more and more of a focus.

Cooper was the first to join an organized football team. Within a year, he showed such promise as a wide receiver that he stopped playing other positions. With that kind of talent, it was no wonder Peyton really looked up to him. "Being the middle child, too, I felt was lucky, to have an older brother, Cooper, to look up to," Peyton said to the *Academy of Achievement*, "and a younger brother, Eli, that looked up to me." Eli did look up to his older brothers, but as the baby of the family he was also the closest to his mother. Olivia took the toddling Eli on many shopping trips to keep her youngest son away from his rambunctious brothers when things got too crazy around the house.

That quality time spent with his mother left an impression on Eli. Sure, he had to put up with the "girly" stuff that his mother enjoyed, but it also meant he got to spend a lot more time with Olivia than his brothers. After a while he even began to enjoy shopping, especially when they went to antique stores. "The first couple of times it wasn't because I wanted to," Eli said to the *New York Times* about their antiquing trips. "It was just because she wanted to go shopping and there was nobody to watch me, so I had to tag along. But after I went a couple of times, I started to enjoy it." He and his mother grew so close during their time together that they still enjoy antiquing together even now. "I'd say I was a momma's boy," Eli said later to AOL Sports. "I'm not ashamed of it. I don't think that's a bad thing."

It might seem strange that such a rough-and-tumble football star is really a big softy at heart, but Eli was always laid-back. In fact, that is how he got his nickname, "Easy." He took after easy-going Olivia, unlike his mischievous brothers. "I was always kind of the quiet one, the shy one," Eli recalled to the *New York Times*. He's proud when people tell him that he reminds them of his mom. After all, she was always the glue that held the Manning clan together. "Growing up, we would have been lost and clueless without her," Eli explained to the *New York Times*. "She ran the household and was our biggest supporter."

Peyton, unlike his younger brother, was closest to his father. "He was always very helpful and supportive and I think that's still today why I have a love for football, because it was fun for me as a kid," Peyton said on PeytonManning.com. "I've always had a true love for sports and I think that's because of the way my dad handled things." All three boys loved playing football with their father, but they loved his stories about playing pro ball just as much. Archie's stories weren't just to entertain his sons, though. Archie wanted to teach his boys important life lessons. One moment stood out in particular for Peyton. Archie had taken a clipping out of a newspaper and brought it home for his son. It read, "Pressure is something you feel only when you don't know what you are doing." They were the words of Chuck Noll, the legendary coach of the Pittsburgh Steelers. Noll definitely knew what pressure was; he had taken his team to four Super Bowl victories. Their father's lessons would definitely serve Peyton and Eli well as they geared up for the next challenge in their young lives—school.

# CHAPTER THREE
## School, Success, and Struggles

Archie Manning finally retired from professional football in 1985 after the Houston Oilers traded him to the Minnesota Vikings. He finished with 2,011 completions, the seventeenth best record in NFL history at his retirement, despite his teams winning only a third of their games. He never played on a team that reached the playoffs, but to this day Archie Manning remains wildly popular in the south. To his boys, it was like having a superhero as a father.

Still, Archie couldn't fix everything for his sons, and he wouldn't have wanted to. He wanted his sons to make their own mistakes and become better men because of it. One of the biggest lessons Archie taught them was that football was great, but academics always come first. It was sometimes tough for the energetic boys to buckle down and study when the football field was calling, but they never slacked off.

"I did like school," Peyton said to the *Academy of Achievement*. "I worked hard in school. I *had* to work hard in school. It didn't come naturally to me, and I could never not study for a test and expect to do even average. I was a grinder, as you would say. I might not study until that morning, but I'd get up at 5:00. I'd have to. I'm a preparation guy." Peyton may not have been a straight-A student, but he always got his work done and was well-behaved. "I was taught at an early age about having a work ethic," Peyton continued.

That work ethic worked wonders for Peyton's education, but despite working hard himself, Eli struggled more than his brothers with school. Eli was quiet and a little sensitive about having a famous father and two charismatic and popular older brothers. He would often let teasing or questioning from his classmates distract him. Even though his dad was retired, Eli thought people looked at him as just "Archie Manning's Son."

Archie tried to keep his family as normal as

possible. "We ate dinner as a family, always had to get up for breakfast and eat breakfast as a family," Peyton said to the *Academy of Achievement*. "My dad used to read a daily devotional to the family. They just tried to keep things normal."

Autograph seekers were everywhere, though, and a family outing could get strained when dozens of people would crowd around Archie. Peyton thrived on all of the fan attention and used it to his advantage, as he explained to the *Academy of Achievement*. "It may have motivated me to work a little harder. I knew people were always looking at me, so it made me kind of think twice about the things that I did."

But Eli couldn't just shake it off like his brothers. He began having more and more trouble with his schoolwork, especially with reading. "As a child, it's embarrassing and frustrating," Eli explained to the *New York Times*. "They call on students to read out loud in class and it's one of those deals where you're praying the whole time that they don't call on you." The more behind Eli fell, the harder he found it to ask for help.

By the time he was in the fourth grade, Eli's parents decided to make some changes. They transferred Eli to another school, and Olivia began tutoring Eli herself before and after school to make sure that he got caught up and didn't fall behind again. "She worked with me and stayed patient. Her laid-back attitude and her soft Southern drawl helped me keep calm about it. She's the one who kept telling me it would all work out and it did," Eli told the *New York Times*. Eli slowly began to catch on. He worked incredibly hard and his reading improved. Soon he was no longer embarrassed to read in front of his classmates.

Meanwhile, Cooper Manning started classes at Isidore Newman High School and was making a name for himself on the football field. He quickly became a starter on the varsity squad. Scouts began to show up at the games, and with Cooper's numbers to back him up, it looked as if he was guaranteed to play college football when he graduated. It certainly helped that Newman had a well-known reputation for having a very strong football program. With lots of tradition and titles, Newman was a magnet for football talent, and playing with the best made Cooper an even better player.

Still in middle school, Peyton set his sights on playing ball for Newman when he made it to high school. Peyton's love for football had been growing since he was little and he had settled upon a very big goal for himself—he wanted to play for the NFL, just like his dad. Archie had been recently hired as a color commentator for the Saints, and Peyton got to tag along and watch NFL practices and games. Peyton soaked in everything he could while watching, but he got most of his inspiration from watching Cooper play. Peyton knew he'd have to step up his game to play on the varsity team with Cooper, so he began badgering his father for help and advice.

"I wasn't a big advocate of organized football for kids. I was scared of that," Archie said to the *New York Post*. "I never coached. I never tried to be their offensive coordinator." Archie may not have wanted to coach, but he didn't shy away from helping when Peyton asked. "I never pushed him into football," Archie Manning explained to *USA Today*. "I didn't try to mold him into a quarterback in my own image. I feel very strongly about not interfering. I don't want to get into being around practices or coaches. I'll be his father and that's it." So Archie didn't help his sons as a former professional player, he helped them as a father. He taught Cooper how to catch a pass on the run, how to read formations, how to get open, and how to dance past defenders. Then he gave Peyton advice on quick snaps, long balls, calling plays, and the basics of quarterbacking. Later, Archie would teach the same kind of moves to Eli.

When Peyton began his freshman year at Newman, people wondered if the Manning magic could strike twice. Cooper was one of the strongest receivers the team had had in years, but Peyton was different from his brother. He didn't want to catch balls—he wanted to throw them. When asked which positions he wanted to play, Peyton wrote down "defensive back" and "quarterback." Peyton knew that becoming the varsity starting quarterback wasn't going to be easy. He made the team and practiced the entire summer before ninth grade, but unfortunately he didn't get to play much in his first year. He was a freshman, after all. So he had to watch from the bench as Cooper and the rest of Newman High lit up the gridiron.

That's not to say that Peyton just stood on the sidelines. He was eager to please and volunteered to help wherever he could, which gave him extra chances to learn from Frank Gendusa, Newman's head football coach. Peyton was also involved in a variety of school activities and made a lot of friends. He was a gifted all-around athlete and he played basketball for two years and started as the shortstop for the baseball team.

As much as he loved baseball, football was Peyton's real passion. He wanted nothing more than to be a starter at Newman, and he really focused the bulk of his attention on that. He gave it his all during the regular season and trained extra-hard the entire summer after his freshman year. "I was kind of ahead of the curve as a high school kid, as far as off-season workouts as a football player," Peyton said to the *Academy of Achievement*. "Most kids, they play football when football season starts, but I was throwing pass patterns with my receivers in May, June, and July."

Peyton's hard work paid off in his sophomore year. His coaches saw how much Peyton trained, and he was given the opportunity to start as quarterback. From the start, he blew everybody away. Newman High went 12-2 overall and advanced to the state semifinals that year, matching its previous best record. With Peyton as quarterback and Cooper as wide receiver, Newman posted its best numbers in years. One of the unexpected benefits of that season was that Cooper and Peyton grew closer than they had ever been before. "That year made us buddies," Cooper explained to *Sports Illustrated*.

Eli wasn't in high school yet, but he never missed a game. Watching his brothers play really motivated Eli. He'd always loved football, but seeing his brothers on the field made him start taking football seriously. He had never wanted to be compared to or lumped in with his brothers, but he finally realized that he could play football and still maintain his individuality. With that revelation, Eli began focusing on football and trying to get ready for his own chance to try high school ball.

Unfortunately for the Manning family, something was about to happen that would change the way that they looked at family, hope, and football forever.

# CHAPTER FOUR
## Fighting Through the Pain

Near the end of his senior year, Cooper Manning began to complain of numbness in his hands and fingertips. It wasn't much more than an annoyance at first. Cooper wasn't in any pain, and even though he found himself dropping balls that he never would have in the past, he ignored it. Eventually, though, the numbness got worse and Cooper began to have trouble doing simple things like holding a pencil or picking up his backpack. He had to see a doctor.

The diagnosis was devastating: Cooper had spinal stenosis. His spine was narrowing, pinching off his nerves as it grew thinner and thinner. Eventually, without treatment, it would cause intense pain and possibly paralysis. Cooper's case wasn't life-threatening unless his body was put under a lot of undue stress, like playing football, for example. The doctors had to operate to fix the problem as soon as possible. Cooper went into the three-hour surgery in 1993. When it was done, his left leg was numb and his right leg was almost as bad. He had to go through months of grueling physical therapy to even walk again. It was a very difficult time for the entire family, but they were all grateful that it wasn't worse. Cooper could have been paralyzed at any time from even a minor hit on the field.

Unfortunately, Cooper would never be able to return to football. His career was over before it had really begun. "It was terrible; I had been playing football since fifth grade," Cooper said to NFL.com. "Suddenly they tell you you can't play anymore. I had to struggle with it for a while." Cooper was devastated, but he tried to make the best of his situation, and the next fall he went on to college at the University of Mississippi.

Peyton and Eli were both impressed with their brother's strength and positive attitude, and it showed them how lucky they really were. "Cooper's situation made me realize how important it is to maintain your priorities," Peyton explained to *USA Today*. "Faith, family, education—everything else is after that. It made me appreciate every single game, every single practice, and treat it as if it's my last. Every game, I'm always thinking of him. I want to do well; I know he's watching."

The realization that it could all be over in an instant inspired Eli to work harder than ever at football. He went to all of Peyton's games, not just because he was a part of the family, but also so he could learn from watching his brother. When Peyton dropped back for a pass, Eli watched how he did it. When Peyton used fancy footwork to shed defenders, Eli studied how he moved. Lessons and advice from Archie were great, but watching Peyton in action really brought the finer points of the game to life.

Eli really couldn't have chosen a better role model. Peyton's numbers just kept getting better. In his junior year, Peyton led his team to an 11-2 finish and into postseason play. His senior year was even more spectacular; Peyton passed for 2,500 yards and thirty touchdown passes while Newman won every regular season game on its schedule. Peyton finished his high school career having thrown over 7,200 yards and ninety-two touchdown passes. He had taken his team as far as the state semifinals, and even though they hadn't won a state title, he had proven to himself that he could lead a team. He had pushed himself and succeeded beyond almost everybody's expectations. Everybody's, that is, except his own. "The thing that gives me peace of mind at night after a game, or after a season, is that I knew that I did everything that I could to get ready to play that game. I couldn't have prepared harder," Peyton explained to the *Academy of Achievement*.

That kind of preparation made Peyton really stand out to the scouts who had so recently been following Cooper's career. Peyton was named the Gatorade National Football Player of the Year for Louisiana, and there were a lot of colleges that wanted a quarterback just like him. Peyton was definitely up for the challenge—he just had to pick the right school. Most fans were expecting Peyton to follow in his father's and older brother's footsteps and attend Ole Miss, but a recruiting scandal had shaken the school and tainted a large number of players there already. Peyton was unsure about Ole Miss, although the school definitely wanted him. "Some of my buddies have called and said, 'You make him [Peyton] go to Ole Miss,'" Archie Manning told *Sports Illustrated*. "They're real hard-core about it. And though I'm sure they mean well, they aren't thinking about what they'd do if Peyton was their son."

Choosing a college was the biggest decision that Peyton had ever had to make. He was serious about playing in the NFL someday, and his college choices would play a big role in reaching that dream. Peyton wanted to make a name for himself all on his own and he was worried about family comparisons overshadowing his own contributions at Ole Miss. "I kind of had the feeling that if I went to Ole Miss, I'd be an instant celebrity without doing anything," Peyton said. "Mississippi people think I'm a good quarterback, but I could never live up to how good they think I am." So Peyton looked at all of his options and eventually chose the University of Tennessee. It was a surprise to lots of people, but Peyton was sure it was the right choice for him.

UT had a strong football program, but it also had a good academic environment. It was an old

Southeastern Conference (SEC) team with a long tradition of football victories, and the school welcomed Peyton with open arms. According to Peyton in his interview with the *Academy of Achievement*, Archie cautioned Peyton to keep his feet on the ground. "You better work harder in college than you did in high school to make it in college, and if you get to pro ball, you better work a lot harder than you did in college, to make it harder than that, if you want to excel at the pro level." So Peyton entered school prepared to work harder than ever to stay at the top of his game.

It wasn't going to be an easy road. Peyton's freshman year saw him sitting on the bench behind Jerry Colquitt and Todd Helton, two experienced quarterbacks who were expected to play for the entire season. In a sea of orange and white uniforms, Peyton was just getting warmed up. People knew him, of course, but he wasn't a superstar quite yet. He practiced and worked out harder than he ever had before, and when Colquitt and Helton went down with injuries, Peyton was more than ready to take over the 1-3 Tennessee Volunteers.

Peyton wound up taking them to an 8-5 record that year. It was good enough to land the team in a bowl game and Peyton in the hearts of UT's many, many fans, even though he was still a little inexperienced. "It was a slow process," Peyton admitted to the *Daily Beacon*. "The more games I played, the more experience I got. I feel I gained more leadership with the players. I could see them looking at me with a different look, which made me feel good. I felt like I had to earn their respect."

Peyton did manage to find some time for old-fashioned college fun. He played practical jokes on his teammates, attended campus events, and just enjoyed being a college student. He also made time to participate in local charity work, like the Multiple Sclerosis Read-a-thon. "It was doubtful at first because of his schedule and his prior commitments," Angela Whitaker, the special events coordinator for the East Tennessee chapter of the National Multiple Sclerosis Society, said to the *Daily Beacon*. "He was very interested. He said it was something he really wanted to do." Peyton always believed in giving back to his community, and that would carry over to when he was playing in the NFL. It was hectic at times to balance being a college football star, attending classes, and helping out in the community, but Peyton was determined to do it all.

One thing Peyton wasn't doing during college was dating UT girls. He had already met the girl of his dreams—his girlfriend, Ashley Thompson. Peyton's next-door neighbor from childhood had introduced him to Ashley the summer before he went to college. She was going to the University of Virginia, but the couple continued to date long-distance, talking on the phone often and visiting whenever they could. Ashley was one of the most supportive people in Peyton's life. "The way I really help Peyton is that I don't demand a lot of his time," Ashley admitted to *Indianapolis Woman* magazine. "He's willing to give it, but I'm not the type of person that is nagging on him. I think that helps him. He's able to do what he needs to do and I'm very independent. I do a lot of my own things."

Ashley majored in finance and marketing at UVA while Peyton finished up at UT. Eventually, with Peyton's support, she became a successful real estate broker. The two continued to date after college and eventually married in 2001 after almost eight years together. Ashley was the perfect match for Peyton. She was independent and successful, and she always supported and encouraged her husband. "I like to stay out of the spotlight," Ashley told *Indianapolis Woman* magazine. "People may think I am aloof, but I'm not, and I am not shy by any means, but I always let Peyton shine."

And shine he did. Peyton's sophomore year was even better than his freshman year, and he attributed it all to hard work. "I worked out with some guys from New Orleans that play in the pros; some defensive backs from the Patriots and Cardinals and some receivers from the Colts and Buccaneers," Peyton said to the *Daily Beacon*. "It's really helped me out because I've been playing with the same level of speed that we have here at UT. It's helped me stay in shape and keep my timing this summer. It's paid good dividends for me."

With Peyton at UT and Cooper at Ole Miss, Eli was left alone in the spotlight at home, and he flourished without the constant pressure of his brothers' success hanging over his head. Peyton still visited often and never failed to give his little brother a hard time, but Eli was coming into his own and began to stand up for himself more. He even took over Peyton's old room! "Early on, I'd give it back to him," Eli said to the *Associated Press*. Later, as he explained to the *Associated Press*, "I finally felt I could stand up to him, so we'd get in a wrestling match. Not a real fight, but a wrestling match. I was finally able to defend myself and I said, 'I'm not going to give it up that easily.'"

During that time, Eli started high school at Newman, just like his two brothers before him. He couldn't completely escape their reputation, but being so much younger did help distance Eli from Peyton and Cooper. "We had Eli kind of alone for five years," Archie said to the *New York Times*. Still very close to his mother, Olivia and Eli began a weekly ritual that meant a lot to Eli. Once a week, just the two of them would go out to dinner. They went to their favorite restaurants: Casamento's for oyster po' boys; Figaro's for pizza; and Joey K's for fried catfish. "I got to know more about her," Eli said to the *Seattle Times*. He didn't have to shout over his brothers and he got to listen to a new perspective on life. "She told stories about growing up or about college. It kind of helped me get my stories out." With more focused attention from his parents and coaches, Eli was able to find out who he was, both on and off of the football field.

Eli had always been the laid-back Manning brother, but once he reached the high school level, his competitive nature began to emerge. He began working out and training nonstop, and practicing whenever he finished his schoolwork. He kept up an active social life and had plenty of friends, but football was his main focus. He wanted to make the Newman varsity team, and when tryout sign-ups were posted, Eli gave it all he had. "Easy" wasn't so easygoing anymore. He wanted to play football. And he wanted to show Louisiana what *Eli* Manning could do.

# CHAPTER FIVE

## A Brand-new Eli

Eli made the varsity squad that year, but only as a backup quarterback. He didn't let that discourage him, though. Eli studied the starters, learned from their mistakes, and stayed sharp for the times late in the games when he would be put in. "He's laid-back but I wouldn't be fooled by that," Newman High athletic director Billy Fitzgerald told the *New York Daily News*. "He is not going to growl and make faces like somebody else might but he is just as competitive. He doesn't like to lose." And Fitzgerald should know; he coached Eli on the varsity basketball team, too.

Eli's new focus on the field helped with his schoolwork, as well. He had always had to put more effort into his education than most kids, but now that he had something to work for, it was getting easier to stay ahead—which isn't to say that he didn't have fun on the side. "He enjoys life," said Sheila Collins, Eli's calculus teacher at Newman, to the *New York Daily News*. "There was a little devilment in him."

In addition to athletics, Eli discovered his theatrical side in high school. He loved singing and classical music, and he was quite the class clown. His favorite show at the time was *Seinfeld* and he used to quote lines from the *Saturday Night Live* skit, "Deep Thoughts by Jack Handey," all of the time. His senior inscription in the yearbook was an inspirational saying followed by one of Handey's "deep thoughts": "Broken promises don't upset me. I just think, why did they believe me?"

Coach Gendusa, the head football coach, explained it all for WLTV: "Cooper is a great guy, the class clown, he always kept things lively. Then you had Peyton who was serious as a heart attack." Both had their own personalities, and Gendusa had to coach them differently because of it. Then along came the other Manning brother. "And Eli," Gendusa remembered, "was laid-back and relaxed."

When his sophomore year rolled around, things

began to really click for Eli on the football field. He had been working out all summer, and a growth spurt put him over six feet tall. His passes were more accurate, his play-calling was more assured, and Eli was ready for anything that might come his way. His coaches saw these changes, and by the beginning of the season, Eli was starting as quarterback for the varsity squad, just like his brother had. Football really was in the Manning's blood.

"There was a time," Olivia told the *New Orleans Times-Picayune*, "when Archie would be at a Newman [high school] game on Friday, a Tennessee game [during Peyton's college years] on Saturday, and a Saints game on Sunday, when he was part of the broadcast team. One of us, usually both of us, have been to every football game our sons have played in going back to high school."

With Eli as the quarterback of the varsity squad, Newman had another strong year in the standings. Eli made 139 of 245 passes for 2,340 yards and twenty-four touchdowns. Newman made it into the playoffs, and most of that had to do with Eli's strong guidance and never-give-up attitude. Eli was proving to be just as great a quarterback as Peyton had been in high school.

Peyton, meanwhile, was surpassing all expectations at the college level. He led the Tennessee Volunteers to four straight bowl games. That included an SEC championship and some serious contention for the national title. "It has been very rewarding to get on the field and to play as a freshman in the best conference in America," Peyton enthusiastically told the *Daily Beacon*.

Archie had been admired during his playing days, but Peyton's popularity was reaching rock-star proportions. He probably could have entered the NFL Draft after his sophomore year. After all, there were plenty of NFL teams desperate for a good quarterback, even one as young as Peyton. But Peyton made the decision to stay at college and earn his undergraduate degree before joining the NFL. "I just thought a lot about it. I prayed a lot about it. I sought a lot of advice from my dad. My dad got me some phone numbers of some guys that I wanted to call, some other athletes that had been in that situation, some that stayed, some that went, and talked about, 'Hey, I regretted it,' or 'No, I did the right thing, I left early.' So I formed kind of a pros and cons list. I like to write things down. I'm kind of a note-taker. I think writing things down creates that blueprint that guides you through the ups and downs of life, and I just made my decision," Peyton explained to the *Academy of Achievement*.

When Peyton graduated from UT, after finishing his senior year with an 11-2 record, he had become the top passer in UT history. He had accumulated 11,201 yards and eighty-nine touchdowns. It was one of the best showings of any quarterback in the history of the SEC. There was a lot of buzz surrounding Peyton when it came time for the NFL Draft. In 1998, the entire family flew up to New York City, where the draft has been held every year since 1965, to support Peyton. Everyone was excited and nervous at the same time.

Peyton was definitely the most nervous. Playing in the NFL was his dream, and he was anxious to discover which team he would end up on. There were rumors swirling that Peyton would be chosen first, but he tried not to make any assumptions. A first overall draft pick comes with a lot of pressure. The team with the first draft pick is always the worst team in the NFL standings. Their need for help to stay afloat is why they get first choice of the eligible amateur players.

In 1998, the Indianapolis Colts had first pick. The franchise was an old one, originally based in Baltimore and established in the 1950s from the remains of the Dallas Texans. They had gone on to be one of the NFL's powerhouse teams for the next twenty years, winning the NFL championship in 1958, 1959, and 1968, and winning the Super Bowl in 1970, with an additional three division titles in the mid-1970s.

The Colts run of good luck had ended since landing in Indianapolis in 1984. It had been a controversial move for fans, and the team had left its success somewhere in their old Baltimore offices. They had secured only three playoff appearances since and had only won three games out of sixteen the previous season. They had to make their first choice wisely, since they were counting on that player to help pull them out of their slump.

The 1998 draft was full of promising players. Peyton was one. Ryan Leaf, a prominent quarterback from Washington State University, was another. To many, he seemed like a safer bet than Peyton to make it big in the NFL. Ryan was bigger, faster, and stronger than Peyton and had done just as well at Washington State as Peyton had at Tennessee. But the Colts were looking for someone special. "I looked at Manning and I knew I was getting a leader who could put this team on his back for 15 years," Colts President Bill Polian said to the *New York Times*. When the draft began, Polian took to the stage and announced that the Colts were choosing Peyton Manning.

A thousand flashbulbs went off. Peyton stood up from his table and hugged his parents and his brothers. It was a stunning moment, and as Peyton walked to the stage, he seemed both proud and a bit dazed. He threw on his new Indianapolis Colts jersey, stood for pictures, and realized that he had achieved his dream. The Colts had chosen him out of thousands of other strong players for their NFL team, and they were hoping that he would be able to take them back to the championship circle. "I'm really honored that I was the No. 1 pick and that the Colts put their faith in me. I hope to make them happy that they chose me," Peyton explained to the *Daily Beacon*.

It turned out to be a good choice. There were other future hall-of-famers in the draft that day, but Peyton would prove to be the most famous. His hard work had paid off, and he was well on his way to achieving his new goal—playing in the Super Bowl. "I was drafted," Peyton would later remember while talking to *Business Today* magazine. "I have a responsibility to my owner, to my general manager, president, to our head coach, and to all our fans to be the best player that I can possibly be. That motivates me every day when I'm lifting weights and running sprints [in the off-season with no coaches around]."

Peyton then signed a massive contract for a rookie, the largest in NFL history. He hadn't played in a single pro game and he was already a millionaire. Polian based Peyton's large salary on the hope that Peyton was going to be a real leader.

The Colts and the city of Indianapolis were banking on Peyton stepping into the shoes of other famous Colts quarterbacks, like Johnny Unitas. But not everyone had Polian's faith in Peyton. His first press conference that day was a blur of questions. Could he save the Colts? Would he exceed his father's career? What did he expect out of the NFL? But the first question reporters asked was, "What are you going to do with all of that money?"

"I'm going to earn it," Peyton answered simply. And was he ever.

# CHAPTER SIX
## The Mannings Take Off

While Peyton was gearing up for the NFL, Eli was facing his own set of pressures at home. He was being heavily recruited by college scouts and his performances junior and senior year on the field had made him a football celebrity around town. "It was nice to see him break out of his shell," Peyton told the *Associated Press*. "I kind of saw it from afar." By the time he was finished at Newman High, Eli would throw for a total of 7,389 yards and over eighty-nine touchdowns. His entire family was proud of his achievements, and they supported him as he made the difficult decision about where to go for college. Eli pretty much had his choice of schools across the country, but he didn't always see himself the same way that everyone else saw him. "I was unsure of myself coming out of high school," Eli said to the *New York Times*. "I had doubts because of all the things that Peyton had accomplished. I didn't think I was as good as him."

Comparing himself to his brothers had always chipped away at Eli's self-confidence. After all, it wasn't easy to live up to a NFL-star father, a high school football hero oldest brother, and the number-one draft pick in the country—all while still in high school yourself! So when David Cutcliffe, Peyton's former offensive coordinator at Tennessee, called to recruit him, Eli had some reservations. But Cutcliffe had moved on from Tennessee and become the head coach for Ole Miss. He invited Eli to come visit and check out Ole Miss's summer football program. Eli didn't want to be compared to his brothers and father throughout college—which would be hard to achieve at Archie and Cooper's alma mater working with Peyton's former coach! But Eli was more than impressed when he made it over to Ole Miss for a visit. "The greatest thing about Coach Cutcliffe is his ability to teach the game of football," Eli told *Star News*. "He works so well with quarterbacks in particular, and teaches you how to lead your team from that position. He works hard, is dedicated and has a passion for winning."

Cutcliffe's passion for winning was only one of the reasons why Ole Miss looked good. Eli remembered how Peyton's game had gone from fantastic "for a kid" to just plain fantastic. He knew that Cutcliffe was a big part of the reason his brother had excelled at the college level. After that visit, Ole Miss became a strong contender in Eli's mind. But another school was courting Eli just as hard— Peyton's alma mater, the University of Tennessee. UT had one of the nation's strongest football programs at the time, but Eli knew that he would automatically be thrust back into Peyton's shadow there. So he made his decision—he was going to Ole Miss.

The University of Mississippi couldn't have been happier. It was one of the most well-respected institutions in the south, with over 150 years of academic and athletic excellence to its name. Archie Manning had been one of Ole Miss's best quarterbacks, leading them to a Sugar Bowl victory during his time there, and they were delighted to continue that legacy with Eli. Ole Miss offered to un-retire his father's number for him, but Eli took number ten instead. He wanted to be his own man and be remembered for his own accomplishments. He didn't want any special treatment, although the school would have been more than happy to give it to him.

Eli was ready to play, but he didn't get to start immediately. In his first season and a half, Romaro Miller started as quarterback in every game. The team had been built up around him, so Eli had to stick to the bench. Cutcliffe kept Eli fresh, though. Miller was a junior and could potentially enter the NFL Draft after the season ended, so Eli needed to be ready. Cutcliffe's strategy was simple—if Ole Miss was winning by enough points, Eli went in to relieve Miller. Cutcliffe had Eli read plays and give his own ideas to Cutcliffe throughout each game. He also had Eli study tape after tape of game footage, reading patterns and looking out for the pitfalls that too many freshman quarterbacks fell into.

When the season ended with a victory at the Independence Bowl, Eli didn't take a break. He kept working extra hard all through the off-season, running drills and working out, both with his teammates and on his own. "I'm trying to win games and to be a better quarterback," Eli said to the *Daily Mississippian*. It wasn't always easy for Eli, but he managed to stay loose despite all of the pressure. He was known on campus for singing at the top of his lungs to karaoke from his dorm room. Eli also wasn't too "cool" to go to parties and hang out with the non-football kids on campus.

It was during one night out that Eli met the love of his life, Abby McGrew. Abby was a pretty southern belle from Tennessee. A former cheerleader from Nashville, she was studying business and fashion. She was the kind of girl Eli wanted to take home to meet his mom, and most importantly, Abby liked him for who he was despite his football skills, not because of them. "She's learning," Eli said to Giants.com. "She's been dealing with it for a while. I don't know if she would watch it if I wasn't playing. She understands it." Being a quarterback didn't get Eli anywhere with Abby. She expected him to act like a gentleman and treat her right.

With Abby by his side, Eli managed to keep it

together despite his worries about the next season. He only had four years to play college football, or so he thought. But Coach Cutcliffe liked Eli's playing and wanted to keep him around, so he redshirted him. That meant Eli had to sit his sophomore year out, but he could still play three more years of college ball once Romaro Miller graduated. Football players can only play football for their first four years of college, unless they are redshirted. Cutcliffe had real faith in the youngest Manning brother, which is why he was willing to redshirt him. So Eli did his best to be patient. All that waiting around did give him plenty of time to keep up-to-date on Peyton's professional career, which was off to an impressive start.

Peyton's passes were sharp, his play-calling was strong, and he was already being looked to as a leader by the rest of his team, despite his young age. Peyton was barely twenty-two, but he had set five different NFL rookie records, including touchdown passes, passing yards, and quarterback rating (a points system that rates quarterbacks based on their statistics). The Colts were still not performing very well—they won only three games in Peyton's first year. But the promise and improvement they showed was enough to keep fans cheering. And, with their record, the Colts would be given first pick in the draft for the second year in a row.

Indianapolis was embracing Peyton for more than just his skills on the field. Almost immediately after joining the league, Peyton set out to give back to his new home. He set up the Peyback Foundation, which gave needy kids from around the country help in sports and in life. St. Vincent Hospital in Indianapolis also got lots of support from Peyton. He gave large donations and often visited to cheer up children staying there. "I had two great parents and a great support system growing up, and I understand that not all kids have those same opportunities," Peyton said to the *Academy of Achievement*.

Not only that, but with Peyton's natural charisma and boyish good looks, his face began to appear all over the country. Since he began playing for the Colts, Peyton has been in multiple advertisments and commercials. DIRECTV had him making fun of his football persona. "I'm into other things," Peyton said in that commercial. "Foreign films, cooking shows . . ." MasterCard had him cheering on average workers, including tailgating for insurance adjusters. He even "learned" how to talk trash for an Xbox 360 commercial. In the ad, Peyton had to act like he was learning how to insult other players from books and audio tapes for *NFL Fever 2003*. Peyton loves his Xbox in real life, too, and he and his brothers play often!

Advertisers couldn't and still can't get enough of Peyton, and neither can fans. SportsBusinessDaily.com even named Peyton Manning the most marketable star in the NFL.

# CHAPTER SEVEN
## Earning It

Peyton had played exceptionally well in his first season, but the team's results were a little disappointing both for Peyton and the people of Indianapolis. Everyone was ready to see Peyton take his team to new heights in his second year. "Manning Is Already the New Colt Hero," wrote Mike Freeman in his headline for the *New York Times*. And he wasn't alone in his opinion. Most sportswriters were saying that Peyton was the next big thing in the NFL. There was a lot of pressure for the team to finally make its way out of its slump. The Colts picked up running back Edgerrin James as their first draft pick that year. Everyone was expecting big things, although many would have probably settled for an 8-8 season.

Peyton gave them more than that. After losing their second game to the New England Patriots, the

Colts never looked back. Opponent after opponent fell in front of them, with Peyton picking up American Football Conference Offensive Player of the Week award for a 400-plus yard game against the San Diego Chargers. The team went on to win eleven of their final twelve games. In just his second year, Manning and the Indianapolis Colts had shattered all expectations. "I just don't think you can play football, and then at the end of the season, just go to the Bahamas and not come back until training camp," Peyton said to the *New York Times*. "All the great players think about football year-round."

At the end of the 1999 season, in Peyton's second year, the Indianapolis Colts had a 13-3 record and were in second place in the American Football Conference (AFC). Unfortunately, the playoffs didn't go so well. The Colts fell immediately to the Super Bowl bound Tennessee Titans, 19–16, in their first playoff appearance with Peyton at the helm. Peyton didn't throw a touchdown pass once that game. Some fans were concerned that Peyton couldn't hold up under pressure. But for the time being, they were more than willing to celebrate getting as far as they had.

Peyton finished the year with 4,135 yards passed and twenty-six touchdowns. He was named to the NFL All-Pro Second-Team and to his first Pro Bowl. Not only that, but for the first time since 1996, the Colts had made the playoffs. Coach Jim Mora's first season of 3-13 was forgotten, and it seemed like he was successfully grooming Peyton to be one of the NFL's top players.

Eli was also excelling. He was working hard at a good school, had a great relationship with a wonderful girl, and also had time to pursue interests outside of football. "I'm comfortable here," Eli said to *Sporting News*. "I can be myself and not have to work at it." The only thing that wasn't going right for Eli was football. He still wasn't playing all that much, but that was about to change. The Rebels had been ranked fairly high all season, finishing 7-5 in the regular season, but in the Music City Bowl, things fell apart. With only a quarter left to play, Coach Cutcliffe found his team down 49–16 in the biggest game of the year. With nothing left to lose, Cutcliffe put Eli in.

It was the chance Eli had been waiting for all

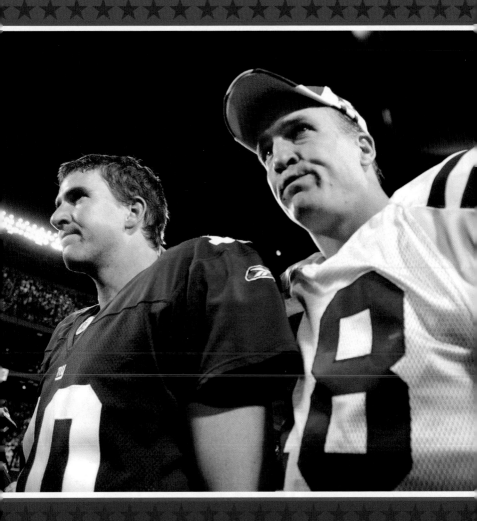

# ELI AND PEYTON MANNING

# ELI MANNING

# PEYTON MANNING

## PEYTON
with his 2007 Super Bowl
Championship trophy.

## ELI
with his 2008 Super Bowl
Championship trophy.

season. In that game, Eli completed twelve of twenty passes for 167 yards and three touchdowns. It wasn't enough for the victory, but his strong performance made everyone look at Eli in a new light. It was all good news for Eli on the gridiron after that. "On the coldest day of David Cutcliffe's life, Eli Manning was red hot," reported the *New York Daily News*.

Eli Manning became Ole Miss's starting quarterback after that. He was a breath of fresh air for the Ole Miss team, and had a very different style than the previous two quarterbacks. He started off at 6-1 during his first season at the helm, and his teammates appreciated his calm leadership style. But a disheartening loss to Arkansas dampened the Rebel's good cheer midway through the season. The game had gone into seven overtimes, and while Eli had thrown for over three hundred yards and six touchdown passes, it wasn't enough. Ole Miss seemed exhausted after that, but Eli held them together to finish at 7-4 for the season.

Despite the disappointing ending, Eli set seventeen records that season, and everyone was excited about the next few years. Ole Miss hadn't been a football powerhouse for a long time, and in a strong conference like the SEC, it took a lot to get noticed. Eli was certainly excited to make his mark on Ole Miss history as a winner. "I try to be a smart quarterback. I'm not the fastest or the best athlete, but if I can know what the defense is doing and stick to my job and what needs to be done I can make the plays needed to move the ball and score," Eli explained to the *Daily Mississippian*.

Both Eli and Peyton were under a lot of pressure to prove themselves. It was up to them to keep up the hard work and pull out strong performances. Eli had to prove he could take his team to a bowl game and Peyton had to prove that his poor performance in the playoffs was just a fluke. Peyton wanted a Super Bowl, and Eli was already starting to focus on making it into the NFL. It wasn't going to be easy, but if anybody could do it, it would be the Manning brothers.

# CHAPTER EIGHT

## Rebel with a Cause

Eli played a total of five seasons with Ole Miss, and he did well in all of them. He led the Rebels to three strong seasons and bowl bids in 2000, 2002, and 2004. He was never a serious contender for the Heisman Trophy like his brother. The Heisman Trophy is an award given to the top college football player as voted on by sports journalists. The journalists who had voted for Peyton a few years earlier thought that Ole Miss's win-loss records weren't strong enough to consider Eli. But that didn't matter. Without the extra pressure of competing for the Heisman, Eli could focus on making the Rebels the best team he could. That focus would eventually pay off in his final season.

In 2003, the senior quarterback proved that he was going to be ready for the NFL, Heisman or not. He passed for 3,600 yards and twenty-nine touchdowns while leading Ole Miss to a 10-3 record, its best showing in thirteen years, and a victory over Oklahoma State at the Cotton Bowl during his final season at Ole Miss. "He knew our road records against teams, who the top 10 high school quarterback prospects were and where they might be going," Cutcliffe said about Eli to the *New York Times*. "His world is football."

Sportswriters and voters from across college football rewarded Eli with honors. He won the Maxwell Award as the nation's best all-around player; the Johnny Unitas Golden Arm Award; the Scholar-Athlete Award from the National Football Foundation and College Hall of Fame; the Radio Socrates Award from *Sporting News*; and, best of all, Eli was named SEC Offensive Player of the Year. It was the biggest honor outside of the Heisman that Eli could have received, and he got the news shortly before he was going to enter the NFL Draft.

But those honors and awards didn't guarantee Eli what he wanted most—a place on an outstanding NFL team and a dazzling pro career. With the draft right around the corner, comparisons between Peyton and Eli were inevitable. After all, they were both quarterbacks who had done well in high school and even better in college. But the pressure just didn't seem to get to Eli. "Eli's got his mother's disposition. I don't know what his agenda is. I know he doesn't worry about a whole lot," Archie told the *New York Times*.

Peyton, on the other hand, was letting the pressure to succeed get to him. Despite an off year in 2001, when the Colts went only 6-10, Peyton performed solidly during the regular season. But when it came time for postseason games, Peyton struggled.

Ultimately, only one game matters in the NFL— the Super Bowl. Peyton, the Colts, and their fans wanted to make it there more than anything, and Peyton was beginning to feel the pressure of failing to achieve that goal. From 1999 until 2002, Peyton only completed one touchdown pass in the playoffs. It took Peyton until the 2003 playoffs to win his first postseason game, a blowout against the Denver Broncos where he threw for 377 yards and five touchdowns. After another strong win against the

Kansas City Chiefs, 38–31, it seemed like Peyton had broken the curse. But that was before the New England Patriots destroyed the Colts in the AFC championship game.

New England had become a thorn in the Colts' side. Led by their superstar quarterback, Tom Brady, the Patriots would go on to win three Super Bowls in four years, setting a record in the NFL. Again and again, the Colts found themselves in a good position at the end of the season, only to lose it all before reaching the Super Bowl. In both 2004 and 2005, it was at the hands of the Patriots. The Colts couldn't even handle the Patriots in the regular season, losing to them eight out of the first ten times they played during Peyton's time as quarterback.

Other than their losses to the Patriots, the Colts were accomplishing a lot. Peyton Manning had taken them to the playoffs more times in his first six years than the Colts had gone without him in the previous twenty years. In that time, the Colts had a total record of 51-29.

But that wasn't enough. Coach Mora was fired early on in 2002 and Tony Dungy, from the Tampa

Bay Buccaneers, replaced him as head coach. Still, some people were looking for someone else to blame. And Peyton, as the quarterback, was an easy target. He had become a television sensation, and some were saying it was distracting him from his work. Tom Brady was also making tons of endorsement deals, as were hundreds of other athletes, but Peyton hadn't won a championship like Tom Brady. "That's football," wide receiver Reggie Wayne said to ESPN after a particularly brutal loss to the Pats after the 2004 playoffs. "Sometimes you play great, sometimes you don't. It's not all on Peyton's hands."

But Peyton took all of the criticism seriously. He blamed himself for his team's losses. Peyton was playing for the Colts fans, and if he was letting them down, then he was ready to take responsibility. "I needed to do my part well today and I didn't do it," Manning said after that 2004 playoff loss. "I feel personally accountable for it and responsible for it." So Peyton kept on working as hard as he could, trying to ignore the media and turn his luck around.

# CHAPTER NINE
## The Big Easy in the Big Apple

"To think about my kid brother who is five years younger than me playing in the league with me is really funny to think about," Peyton Manning admitted to IGN.com. "I remember when he used to play catch with me in the front yard and I was a senior in high school and he was in the seventh grade."

Peyton may have had a hard time believing it, but Eli wasn't a kid anymore. He finished his last football season at Ole Miss in 2003 and signed up for the 2004 NFL Draft. Eli was one of the most talked-about players eligible that year. Draft day was like a zoo that year. General managers were running between tables, trying to trade for a better pick.

The 2004 draft was complicated because the San Diego Chargers and the New York Giants both wanted Eli. Both teams were up for first pick in the draft, but the Chargers won that right in the end. Everyone knew that the Chargers were going to choose Eli, so the Giants would have to be willing to make a major trade if they wanted to steal Eli. Of course, the Giants could have settled for Philip Rivers. Rivers was the quarterback for North Carolina State and was also very promising. He'd led the Wolfpack to four straight bowl games and a Gator Bowl victory over Notre Dame in his senior year. If 2004 had been any other year, Rivers might have been picked first. But no one wanted to be stuck with a bust like former Washington State University quarterback Ryan Leaf, who had been Peyton's competition back in the 1998 draft.

Leaf had left a sour taste in the mouth of many NFL general managers. While playing for the Chargers, he routinely insulted his teammates and coaches. He was moody, difficult to play with, and inconsistent. In just his third start, he completed one pass in fifteen attempts for four yards, and fumbled twice. By the time Peyton was pushing for a Super Bowl, Leaf had retired from football.

The Chargers had learned a valuable lesson and

weren't going to walk away from this draft empty-handed. But the Giants didn't want Rivers to flop in their hands, either. Eli Manning came from a proven football family—it was unlikely that he would fizzle out. And both teams were hungry for a franchise quarterback. The Giants, in particular, were looking to get back into Super Bowl contention and quickly. They had made it for their 2000 season, only to lose 34–7 to the Baltimore Ravens. Their general manager, Ernie Accorsi, had tried to pick up the legendary John Elway in the 1983 draft, but failed. He wasn't about to let another opportunity like that pass him by.

San Diego wasn't listening to Accorsi's trade offers before the draft began. Eli went first overall, just like his brother, with everything from the hugs from his family to the snaps of the cameras. He was going to be a Charger. Within minutes, though, it was clear that something was up. There was a flurry of activity from the Giants table. Eli went to give an interview about being picked first, and then suddenly a reporter gave him the news: The Giants had made a deal. Eli was being traded.

Eli hugged his mom, his agent, and his brother, and was then swarmed by the press. Of course, Eli was a man of few words when he was asked about his reaction. "I'm happy," he said to the reporters. When the noise died down, Eli officially became a New York Giant. Accorsi had picked Rivers and then immediately traded him and three other draft picks to the Chargers for the rights to Eli. It was a high price to pay, but Accorsi and many others thought it was worth it. "This is great. This is fabulous. What a happy day," Olivia said to the *San Diego Union-Tribune*. "We're going to have fun in New York tonight."

In an interview for DIRECTV, Peyton got to ask Eli how he felt about being picked first in the draft. Despite his brother's teasing and jokes, Eli said, "It's a great honor to be the number-one pick. It's something . . . I've worked really hard to get to this position, put in the names of a lot of great players." Eli was all business. Well, not entirely. Asked by Peyton if certain "rumors" were true that Eli considered himself better-looking than his older brother, Eli smiled. "It is a bold statement, and obviously, that is my opinion, and I feel very strongly about that opinion."

It was a great day for Eli, after all, and he could joke around as much as he wanted. He was moving to the world's biggest stage to play football for an enormous contract. He was a superstar. Within hours of his trade, New Yorkers were already buying Eli Manning customized Giants jerseys.

Eli tried to remain focused on the future and his game despite the hype. "I think the biggest challenge will be getting used to the NFL, the speed of things, the complexity of defenses, learning a new offense, and trying to get into a rhythm with the receivers," Eli said at his post-draft press conference. "There's a lot of things that are not easy, but I think you've just got to work hard and be determined to get better."

But Eli had no idea what he was in for. The New York media is well-known for being hard on its players. Alex Rodriguez faced a lot of angry articles and headlines as soon as he began to stumble as a New York Yankee, just like Reggie Jackson and Mickey Mantle before him, despite all of their usually stellar skills. For a city that loved winners, nothing short of perfection was good enough, especially when it came to football.

The New York Giants had been an up-and-down team since they started playing. The team had won Super Bowls in 1987 and 1991, plus numerous championships in the days before the AFC and NFC championships. They had also gone through several losing seasons right before they signed Eli on. The Giants also already had a quarterback— Kurt Warner. Warner had won a Super Bowl with the St. Louis Rams only a few years before. The management and fans of the Giants were worried that Warner and Eli wouldn't get along. Luckily, Kurt was more than happy to help tutor his eventual replacement. "Hopefully what I had the last six years is going to catapult me quicker to the position I want to be in, that leadership role I know guys are looking for when you come in with the success that I've had," Warner said to the *New York Times*. He was getting older and he knew some young gun was always going to be after his job. "It kind of comes with the territory."

Eli, for his part, knew his role as a backup,

though he definitely didn't want it to stay that way. "I'm going to go out there and do what I can to be the starting quarterback," Eli said to the *New York Times*. "If that doesn't happen, I'm not going to be disappointed. I'm not going to consider it a failure. I will just keep working hard."

Warner began instructing Eli on the finer points of quarterbacking. Not throwing, or play calling, or anything like that; Eli had those things down already. Warner taught Eli how to keep up with the pace of the game on the professional level. Everybody was fast in the NFL. Certain plays and dodges that might have worked in college just didn't cut it in the pros. From the bench, the youngest Manning brother was anxious to get out on the field, but he didn't rush it. He wanted to stay in the league for a long time, and with a mentor like Warner helping him get his feet wet, Eli was prepared to wait a bit and test the waters.

Backing up wasn't new to Eli. After all, he had done it in high school and college in his first years. Eli remembered all of the lessons that he'd learned along the way and began watching how the game was played in the NFL. His career depended on it. And like Peyton before him, he discovered it was way beyond his imagination.

First, there was the glamour of it all. People were desperate for autographs. Eli had once walked down the streets of New Orleans like any other person. Now that he was in New York, he couldn't go anywhere without being recognized. People wanted him in commercials, TV shows, movies, and on gigantic cardboard cutouts in their rooms. He met celebrities and went to huge Hollywood parties. A year before, Eli had been the big man on campus. Now he was the big man in the Big Apple, and he was about to get even bigger.

With Warner at the helm, the Giants were playing well but unevenly. They lost their opening game, then won five of their next six before dropping two tough ones. At 5-4, the Giants were ready to jump to the top or drop to the bottom.

Coach Tom Coughlin was new on the job and wanted to make a bold move. Despite Warner's decent playing, he named Eli Manning the starting quarterback for the tenth game of the season. After all, the Giants didn't really have anything to lose. It looked like the playoffs were beyond them if things continued the way they had been going, so any improvement would be better than nothing.

But Eli was not ready when Coughlin first put him in. He struggled as he adjusted to being an NFL quarterback. The Giants didn't score more than fourteen points for their next four games, and some of the more skittish fans began to get nervous. Was Eli all he was really cracked up to be? After that, Eli had a one-on-one meeting with Coughlin. "Coach, I want to be good," Eli said to him. "I want to be the quarterback of the New York Giants. I want to lead the New York Giants to victory." Coughlin remembered that discussion vividly, even years later at a press conference after the 2008 playoffs. "He was frustrated and hadn't played well. He kind of lost his poise a couple times in that experience and just sat there in my office . . . You saw some of that emotion pouring out of him. He's got it deep inside. He masks it very, very well."

The talk with Coughlin seemed to be just what Eli needed. He regained his confidence, and soon the entire team knew why he was called "Easy." With every game, Eli was picking up more and more of the particulars of his team, seeing how his teammates ran plays, and learning how a defense worked in the pros. By the end of the season, the entire team was behind him. "People around him see what he can do . . . I just spoke to a number of our guys this morning as they left," Coach Coughlin said at the season's wrap-up, according to NFL.com. "That's probably the exciting part is that they now have a pretty good idea over the last three weeks of what this young player is capable of doing." With their support, Eli was living up to his potential. In the last three games of the season, Eli had two great performances in tight losses to the Pittsburgh Steelers and Cincinnati Bengals. The Giants won their last game against an old rival, the Dallas Cowboys. The local media was back to hailing Eli as the next big thing in New York sports.

Fans in New York began to hope, even though the Giants hadn't made the playoffs. Eli was showing progress, and it was only a matter of time until he was rivaling his brother for MVP honors. Peyton had had a rough first year, but by the 2004 season, he had turned the Colts into a monster of a team. Eli was showing just as much promise as Peyton had in his rookie year. He was a millionaire and a household name. Things were looking all right.

At least they were until the summer of 2005. The Manning's hometown was in for a disaster of epic proportions, and nothing in football could compare to the way it would change the lives of everyone from New Orleans, including the entire Manning family.

# CHAPTER TEN

## The Hurricane

Just weeks after the 2005 season started, Hurricane Katrina crashed into the southeastern United States. It had been a small storm that had picked up steam over the Gulf of Mexico, and few people expected it to create the wreckage it did. As it drilled the coast, roofs were torn off buildings, bridges were destroyed, and thousands of people lost their lives. Parts of Mississippi, Alabama, Texas, Florida, and Louisiana were devastated. New Orleans was nearly destroyed completely.

New Orleans is an old port city built almost entirely below sea level. Dams and locks, called levees, keep the waters from the Gulf and nearby swamps from overflowing during storms, but those precautions can only handle so much. As Hurricane Katrina grew in intensity to become a Category 5 storm, the levees broke. In a few days, what had once been a thriving city of almost half a million people was partially submerged under raging waters, with hundreds of thousands of people left homeless.

Both Archie and Olivia were okay, and the Mannings' home, on higher ground, was left relatively untouched, but the rest of New Orleans was either underwater or severely damaged. Camps set up all over the United States took in the homeless. Families were separated and a national emergency was declared for much of the Gulf Coast. When Peyton and Eli heard the news, they were devastated. "The whole town is like family, so it's very much a personal issue," Peyton said to CNN. "It's just different when you have your hometown hit. It just triggers a nerve." Whole neighborhoods vanished. Parts of Eli and Peyton's childhood were gone forever. Suddenly, football seemed unimportant in comparison.

Even with all of the responsibilities of their teams on their shoulders, Peyton and Eli couldn't ignore the situation at home. The brothers dropped everything and delivered over 30,000 pounds of water, Gatorade, baby formula, diapers, and pillows to the people of New Orleans. "We just wanted to do something extra, so we set up this plan to help some of these people," Peyton explained to CNN. "We had no idea what we were going to see, we were just kind of going by reports we've seen on TV. We talked to the Red Cross and asked how could we make an impact in the best way."

They weren't afraid to get their hands dirty, either. Both brothers spent all the time they could in New Orleans, making appearances, helping relief workers, and helping with reconstruction efforts. "I talked to the Red Cross and told them I certainly didn't want to get in the way, but I wanted to do whatever I could to help," Peyton said to CNN. "They said these people are down, so any kind of morale boost we could give would be good for them, too." Having two well-known, hometown football players out there, sweating and working with people who normally watched them on TV, did help boost survivors' spirits. Soon, many other stars and sports figures came to help. Aid flew in from around the United States and the world, both in the form of donations and supplies, as well as manpower. It wasn't just celebrities, though. Eli inspired New Yorkers to open their hearts to the city of New Orleans.

"They have an understanding of what's going on in New Orleans," Eli said to *USA Today*. "Many people have called me and asked what they can do to help." The tragic terrorist attacks of September 11, 2001 were still fresh in New Yorkers' minds. New Yorkers knew how much the nation's support and help had meant to them during their tragedy, and they wanted to help. Eli and Peyton were more than willing to lead the way. The reconstruction of New Orleans became about more than rebuilding a city; it was about a country pulling together and helping people recover after a disaster.

When football called, the Mannings reluctantly went back to their teams. It was their job to play, and the country needed something to cheer for after Katrina. Both Peyton and Eli were inspired by everything they'd gone through recently. They had seen their hometown nearly destroyed, but they'd also watched as hundreds of people came together to help. It was enough to push both Mannings to their best seasons in years.

Kurt Warner left New York to play in Arizona, leaving Eli as the starting quarterback. It was risky to have a rookie starting quarterback like Eli, but Coach Coughlin had faith in Eli. The pressure was on, and Eli had to produce results. The Giants did not disappoint. They won their first two games and never looked back. Eli lead an offense that finished eighth in the NFL in touchdowns, while finishing in the top third in both passing yards and touchdown passes. When the last game was decided, the Giants had finished at 11-5, their best season since going to the Super Bowl in 2001.

Meanwhile, Peyton had his own stellar season. The Colts jumped out of the gate, raring to go, and quickly won their first thirteen games. By the end of the season, Peyton led the Colts to the top of the AFC. Peyton finished second in the MVP voting, won the Walter Payton Man of the Year award, and was nominated in the FedEx Air Player of the Year award. He was also named to the Pro Bowl for the third consecutive year. Unfortunately, neither Manning brother made it to the Super Bowl that year. The Giants had played strong football, but were quickly ousted in the playoffs by the Carolina Panthers. The Colts made it as far as the AFC championship game before the Pittsburgh Steelers squeaked past them on their way to a Super Bowl championship.

Still, it had been a very good football year. Eli was quickly maturing as a player. In just his second season, he finished in the top five quarterbacks in the NFL in touchdowns and yards. He was looking more and more like his older brother every day. And Peyton was doing better and better in every playoff year. Even the critics didn't ride him as much anymore. When they did, he didn't let them get him down. Both brothers had come to realize how little it all mattered in the face of something much, much bigger than football. "It's hard to watch what's happened to the city, people with no place to go, up to their waists in water," Peyton explained in an interview broadcast across the country.

With Super Bowl XL decided for the Steelers, the off-season began, but Peyton and Eli were determined not to let any other opportunities go by.

They worked out, contributed more man-hours to the Hurricane Katrina relief effort, and thought more about the upcoming season. Training camp was only a few months away, and the Manning brothers were ready to prove that everything they had seen and learned had changed their games and their lives for the better.

# CHAPTER ELEVEN
## The Road to Miami

The 2006 season started off like any other, with expectations high for the Manning brothers. Sportscasters expected a by-the-numbers season. The Patriots, the Steelers, the Seahawks, and the Panthers—those were the teams who were going to make it big. That was the forecast, at least.

But after the first week, nothing went according to plan. The Super Bowl champion Steelers only managed to go 8-8 in the season. The Saints, only a year after Hurricane Katrina and a 3-13 season, managed to post their best season ever. The Chicago Bears exploded in the NFC and never looked back. It was a whole new ball game, and one that Eli was enjoying. Thanks to his stellar playing the year before, he was being featured in commercials and ads alongside his older brother. One DIRECTV ad even featured Archie giving tips to the then up-and-coming quarterback Matt Leinart as Peyton and Eli looked on, confused and hurt. "I don't think any of us are going to win an Academy Award or Tony Award for commercials, but we're having a lot of fun," Peyton said, chuckling, to MSNBC. Eli immediately agreed. "Anytime we do something together and especially here just in between takes, we always have a few laughs."

Being brothers meant that Peyton and Eli were always going to be compared to each other. But Eli had changed, and he was finally okay with being compared to his older brother. "For the most part, if I'm being compared to Peyton, I consider that a compliment," Eli said in an interview with *Sporting News*. "He's at the top of his game, and I'm not anywhere near his level right now. But that's the goal, to play at a high level, and he's the guy playing at the highest in the league." If people wanted to compare Eli and Peyton, that was fine with them. Although at the time, Peyton was doing everything he could to stay out of the public eye.

It was amazing how fast it had happened. One day, Peyton was the hero of the Colts. The next, newspapers and fans were calling for his head. When Peyton signed a massive, ninety-eight million dollar contract before the 2004 season, there was grumbling that he hadn't earned it. "Manning: Beating a Dead Horse," wrote one columnist for the *Boston Globe*. "Peyton can't win the big one," reported Nbcsports.msnbc.com. "Until the frenzied final minutes," another journalist recounted for the *Associated Press* on Peyton's play against the Steelers in the 2006 playoffs, "he was mostly a non-factor."

But Peyton wasn't going to let his team down that year. Rolling into another strong start, Peyton led the Colts to nine straight wins to open the season. The Colts finished strong, too, landing a 12-4 record, which was good enough for the top of their division yet again. But the Patriots took the number-one spot in the conference. It looked like another playoff race was going to end up with Peyton watching from home and Tom Brady holding up the Vince Lombardi Trophy. But the Colts weren't going down without a fight.

Their first playoff game was against the Kansas City Chiefs. The Colts beat them 23–8. The critics weren't appeased, but Peyton had gotten his team one step closer to Super Bowl XLI. Next, they played the Baltimore Ravens in a close game. Peyton stumbled a bit but pulled it together to lead the Colts to victory, 15–6. The victory over the Ravens put the Colts in the AFC conference game against their old foes, the New England Patriots. Football experts were predicting another blowout, with the Patriots killing the Colts.

Peyton couldn't have gotten through the pressure without the support of his family. "I don't go around bragging about my children, but he will compete," Archie said of Peyton to *Sports Illustrated*. "There may be days when he throws five interceptions, gets sacked eight or nine times, but he'll keep competing. I've learned that much about him over the years." All of the predictions from before the game haunted the Colts' fans. And when the first half ended with the Colts down 21–6, it seemed like old times all over again.

But like he had all season, Peyton cast aside all doubt and rose to the occasion. With the game on the line, he rallied his troops and stunned the

Patriots. Throwing a touchdown and running for another, Peyton led his team to thirteen points in the second half. The Colts' defense remembered the feeling from their loss to the Steelers a year before and held strong against the number one offense in the league. When the dust had settled after the second half, the score was 38–34. The Colts had finally beaten the Patriots and proven all of their critics wrong.

But Peyton told the *Associated Press* that it wasn't all about him finally succeeding in the playoffs. "I don't play that card. I know how hard I worked this season, I know how hard I worked this week." Peyton had definitely proven himself. The Colts were in the Super Bowl, and Indianapolis had Peyton to thank for it. But it wasn't the end of the season just yet.

On a dreary Sunday in Miami, the Indianapolis Colts met the Chicago Bears in Super Bowl XLI. Rain had turned the field into a muddy mess, but the game went on. It was the Super Bowl, after all, America's biggest sporting event. Tickets were going for thousands of dollars, while commercial time was worth millions. Peyton and the Colts were on the biggest stage of their lives, and if they could turn in one more good performance it would make all of their hard work and struggles worthwhile.

The game started off slowly, but quickly turned into a defensive brawl. Rex Grossman, quarterback for the Bears, fumbled a major play near the end of the half, missing many major targets. Peyton was also shaky, with an interception and only one short touchdown pass to his name. Both defenses, aided by the rain and the mud, were keeping the score low, but they were getting tired.

At halftime, the Colts were leading, 16–14, but the Bears were favored to pull it out. Both teams headed into the locker room as Prince performed the halftime show, but Chicago looked optimistic. After all, Peyton Manning always came up short in big games. Or at least he had in the past. Peyton wasn't about to let his team down this time. This was their chance. The Patriots were already at home, watching the Colts play on TV. If that wasn't a sign, then what was?

After a pep talk, the Colts came out in the third

quarter looking like they'd swallowed lightning. It was the beginning of the end for the Bears, as they only managed to score one field goal for the entire last half of the game. Colts kicker Adam Vinatieri, who had missed a big field goal in the AFC championship the year before, was able to sink two as Peyton kept the offense from turning over any more balls. When defensive end Kelvin Hayden caught an interception from Grossman and ran it back for a touchdown, the Colts momentum was sealed.

By the end of the fourth quarter, the score was 29–17. As the final seconds of the game ticked down, it finally began to sink in. Cheering erupted from the fans, both in the stands and back home in Indianapolis. Super Bowl XLI was over, and the underdog Colts had won. Reporters, fans, and officials stormed out onto the field to take pictures, get interviews, and just be a part of the celebration. Both coaches congratulated each other on the game and the season. The sound was deafening as people swarmed down onto the field. And that wasn't all; it was soon announced that Peyton had been named

Super Bowl MVP. Peyton was thrilled and he had to thank one person in particular before he did anything else. He ran over to his father and gave him a huge hug. Archie had never made it to the playoffs as a player, let alone the Super Bowl. But seeing Peyton fulfill his dream made Archie the proudest that he had ever been in his entire life. "Maybe," Archie Manning said to the *Washington Post*, "there was a little fate there."

Soon afterward, the Super Bowl MVP was everywhere. Peyton waved the green flag for the Indianapolis 500. He and the Colts appeared on a Wheaties box. The "most marketable star in the NFL" even found time to make fun of his various appearances and endorsements on *Saturday Night Live*. Eli was proud of his brother, but he also found all the celebrations a little bittersweet. Eli's 2006 season had not been as great, and even though he was still growing as a quarterback, Eli was facing a lot of criticism. Whether he would be able to weather his storms as well as Peyton had was yet to be seen.

# CHAPTER TWELVE
## The Toughest Year

"I think this has been a difficult year for [Eli]," Coach Coughlin said after the 2006 season ended. "The things that happened with the New York Giants—the expectations being so high." The New York Giants campaign that year had seemed doomed from the start. Tiki Barber, one of the best running backs that had ever played for the Giants, was thinking about retiring. Tom Coughlin's strict workout regimes and coaching skills were under attack from various players and the media. Giants co-owner John Mara was desperate for another Super Bowl ring, no matter what the cost. With their spectacular finish the year before and all the promise that the season held, New York was hoping that its Giants could go deep into the playoffs. And at first, that's exactly what it looked like would happen.

Eli Manning started off the season solidly, taking his team to six wins in its first eight games. Barber was running well, Plaxico Burress was catching, and the defense was on fire. But with eight games left to go, all the wheels fell off of the Giants train. They lost the next four games straight, finishing the season 8-8 and tied with the Packers for the final playoff spot. The Giants only made it to the postseason on a technicality, because of how strong their victories were compared to the Packers' wins.

Eli seemed to have made an about-face since his solid 2005 outing. With eighteen interceptions against twenty-four touchdowns, it hardly seemed like Eli was the same man that the Giants had pinned their hopes on. Even his own teammates were criticizing Eli. Michael Strahan, who had been one of his earliest supporters, was getting restless. "I'm thinking of winning right now," he said to AOL Sports. "They say Eli's going to mature. Well, I need him to mature now."

All of the negativity got to Eli and his team. They weren't prepared for the playoffs and they lost their first game. Playing Philadelphia on the road, Eli looked tired, while his offensive line seemed shattered. The Eagles made short work of the Giants, and at the end of the game, New York had lost, 23–20. The season was over and the Giants said good-bye to Tiki Barber, who retired after that game. It was a sad way to end the year.

Eli knew he had to prove that he was ready for the NFL during his next season by producing the necessary results or risk losing it all. "The only thing that matters is what happens on the field, so I don't pay attention to anything," Eli admitted in his postgame press conference after losing to the Eagles, according to NFL.com. "I don't read into anything or worry about that. My focus is on getting prepared to play."

With his season over, Eli headed back to his parents' home in Louisiana to watch his older brother storm through the postseason. He cheered Peyton on, but anybody who saw him knew that he was disappointed in himself. The New York media and Giants fans were letting him have it, and it seemed to be taking a toll on usually easygoing Eli. Abby and his family comforted him, and Eli eventually got over the loss. It was hard, but looking around the still-rebuilding New Orleans reminded him about the importance of priorities. Cooper hadn't even made it to the NFL; Eli was living out both his own dream and that of his oldest brother.

Super Bowl XLI came and went. Eli sat up in a luxury box, watching as the Colts and the Bears went at it in the rain. Every once in a while, when there was a break in the action, TV cameras would cut to Eli. He looked like he wanted to be down there. And he did. Desperately. While watching his brother at the Super Bowl, something clicked for Eli. "It put a hunger inside me," Eli said to *Sports Illustrated*. He wouldn't let himself get down. He had gotten through tough times before: his grades, high school football, and college football. This was only going to stop him if he let it stop him. He knew he had the strength and the skill to make it. He hadn't worked hard his entire life just to let his dreams slip through his fingers so early on in his career. "You always want to win, but after that I felt like I wanted it even more," Eli said. When the Colts won the Super Bowl, 29–17, it made Eli hungrier than ever to win. Luckily, his next chance was only a few months away.

# CHAPTER THIRTEEN

## A Giant Leader

No one was looking at Eli at the beginning of 2007 season. Peyton and the Colts weren't the center of attention, either. Everybody's eyes were turned to Foxboro, Massachusetts. The loss to the Colts the year before had put Patriots coach Bill Belichick in a bad mood. After signing the talented but stormy Randy Moss, the Patriots steamrolled to a fantastic start. They used the preseason to test out new plays and new players, and when they opened the season, they looked good—better than any team had ever looked, in fact.

Few fans or sportscasters gave any other team much of a chance. Tom Brady was on a record-setting pace, leading his offense to one impressive victory after another. New England outscored its first five opponents 182–65. The Cowboys, the Steelers, the Packers—no one could stop the Patriots. Even

Peyton's Colts floundered after a strong first half in their game, finishing with a score of 24–20. The Patriots finished the season undefeated, the first team to do so since the 1972 Dolphins went 14-0. But the Patriots had played sixteen total games, setting the record for the most games ever won by a regular-season team. Super Bowl XLII didn't seem so much of a destination as a destiny.

"They could be the best team ever," Strahan admitted to Giants.com. "Who knows? . . . I take my hat off to them." For the first time in their lives, the Mannings were thoroughly outshone. Peyton led the Colts to a stellar 13-3 season, but that only got them second place in the AFC. In the playoffs, the Chargers quickly bumped out the Colts. Peyton's dream of a back-to-back championship was over.

Eli faced a much tougher road to the postseason. After starting the season 0-2, Giants fans weren't happy. Coach Coughlin was facing pressure from the media to resign . . . or else. Tiki Barber also didn't have the kindest words to say about his former teammate, calling his leadership qualities "comical" during a *Sunday Night Football* broadcast. But Eli

Manning knew all about pressure, and this time it wasn't getting him down. "It's just one of those deals," Eli said to a group of reporters at a Giants practice, according to NFL.com. "The guy goes to the media and he's got to say stuff. He's been put in a situation where he's got to talk. That's just the way it is. That's the world we live in and you have to deal with it."

Eli was playing it cool. He remembered all of the lessons that his mother taught to him about life and that his father taught to him about football. He had had a bad start, but Eli just worked harder to turn things around. "I just can't tell you how much I appreciate that kind of work ethic because I'm very much the same mode," Peyton said to ESPN at the end of the season. "I think what you put into it is what you are going to get out of it. I can just tell, just being in Indianapolis and from very afar, just how hard he has worked and how much he puts into it and how seriously he takes his profession."

What happened next to the Giants, no one quite knows for sure. Maybe the offense finally started gelling. Maybe the normally strict Coughlin relaxed enough to let his team run the game their way. Or maybe Eli was tired of taking all of the blame. But from the team's third game forward, the Giants didn't slow down. They beat the Eagles, the Jets, the Falcons, the 49ers, and the Dolphins. Their offense was on fire—scoring more than twenty-four points in three of those games—while their defense limited opponents to less than seventeen points on all but one occasion.

Just like the year before, the Giants were 6-2 after eight games, and so Manning wasn't getting too excited. "We want to go out there and play ball and we are not trying to do anything different or change," Eli said to Giants.com before their game against Dallas. "We are going to go in there and try to figure out what kind of game it is going to be, execute our plan, and try to figure out a way to win the game." And win they did. The winning streak continued and the Giants finished up the season 10-6, second in their division behind the conference-best Dallas Cowboys. Even their final season loss to the Patriots couldn't get them down. The Giants had kept the game close against the best team in the NFL, losing 38–35, and Eli outshone his entire team, throwing for four touchdowns and keeping the Giants in it until the final few minutes.

Of course, few outside of New York were talking about the Giants in that game. It was a warm-up game for the Patriots, they said. The Patriots were number one in the league and got to take a week off in the first round of the playoffs. The race for the AFC championship was over, many said. The only question was who the Patriots were to play in the Super Bowl.

That final season match was a warm-up game in a sense, but not for the Giants. The Giants had been pitted against some tough opponents and had to focus on their own games, but nothing could shatter Eli's confidence. The usually quiet quarterback was seen joking around, more relaxed than he had ever been going into the playoffs. The Giants were working together as a team, and Eli was happy to be there. "There has always been a trust between us," wide receiver David Tyree said to *Pro Football Weekly*. "He knows he can throw me the football and I'll be in position where I need to be." "Eli from the beginning through now is the same with me," Brandon Jacobs said on the same day. "Everyone else thinks that he is not a leader and says all these different things about him—say he doesn't get excited, his reactions are terrible, so on and so forth. Well, the guy hasn't thrown an interception in the last month."

The Tampa Bay Buccaneers tried to put a stop to the Giants success, but failed. Eli led his team to a 24–14 win in Tampa, and just like that, he had his first playoff victory. Drenched in sweat, an elated Eli still made time for a postgame wrap-up with the press. "We have been in the playoffs the last three seasons, and I haven't played particularly well in the two games before. Just to come here and play well, give our team a chance to win the game and make some big plays, that was quite a situation to be in . . . But now you can't be just satisfied with what you're doing. It's about the bigger picture and keeping this thing going."

That was for sure. Up next were the Dallas Cowboys, the old rival of the Giants. The Cowboys were the top-ranked team in the NFC and had only lost twice at home during the year, and one of those times was to the Patriots. Eli ignored the forecasts of a Cowboy blowout and took charge. Trailing 17–14 with one quarter left, Eli drove his team down the field, allowing running back Brandon Jacobs to score from the one-yard line. The Cowboys tried to mount an offense, but it was too late; the Giants defense held on. The final score was 21–17, Giants. The teams rushed onto the field, and Eli—with his two touchdown passes—was seen grinning from ear to ear amidst the chaos. Brett Favre and the Green Bay Packers were all that was left between New York and New England for the Super Bowl.

For Green Bay and Favre, it had been a fairy-tale season. No one had predicted that they would go far, but Favre was on his last legs and wanted to go out in a blaze of glory. In what would prove to be his final season, Favre took the Packers to a 13-3 record, good enough for second in the division and home-field advantage in the chilly confines of Lambeau Field for the NFC championship game.

Eli had not done well in cold weather games before. In any case, once again the Giants were seen as the underdog. The Packers were doing everything they could to win. They practiced in the cold to get ready; they tried to keep tickets in the hands of Packers fans; they even called off reruns of *Seinfeld*, Eli's favorite show, from local air before the game. When Jerry Seinfeld heard about that, he sent Manning every DVD from his show. "If they think that's going to mess him up," Strahan said to Gothamist.com, "I should probably move to Green Bay. I could be very successful there with some of my ideas."

Everybody was trying to get into the spirit of the game. The mayors of Green Bay and New York City even made a wager on the game: New York cheesecake against Green Bay cheese-wedge sunglasses. Eli was just trying to keep his mind focused on the game. "I am just looking forward to Green Bay," Eli said to Giants.com. "That is the only thing that matters, what you do next week. The opponent this week is Green Bay, and it is going to be a tough game but we are looking forward to it."

What no one counted on was how much Eli had changed. He wasn't just a kid anymore. He had four full seasons as an NFL quarterback under his belt and was riding a white-hot Giants team. Brandon Jacobs, Plaxico Burress, Amani Toomer, Michael Strahan, and everybody else in the red, white, and blue uniforms were backing him up. "I never doubted myself, and my teammates and coaches haven't doubted me," Eli said in a press conference just days before the Super Bowl. "They have total confidence in me. You need to have a great supporting cast and I've had that between my teammates, coaches, family and having Peyton there."

With temperatures below zero degrees and snow flurries buffeting the field, the Giants and the Packers clashed. The game was an even matchup, with the lead seesawing back and forth more than four times. Neither defense was making it easy, and the roar of the crowd and wind made it hard for both teams throughout the entire game.

Eli Manning kept his head, though, and with the aid of hand warmers and lots of communication with his team, he managed to lead his team into overtime. He didn't make any pretty plays and he didn't throw any touchdowns, but he was consistent and hit his targets, and, after an interception by the Giants, he set his team up for the winning score. Through the wind and snow, kicker Lawrence Tynes smashed a ball up into the air and—after what seemed like a full minute—through the uprights.

It had taken four years, but Eli Manning had brought the New York Giants to the Super Bowl. There were celebrations and cheering from the team in the locker room and the fans at home in New York that night, but Eli played it low-key and found Abby on the sidelines. He was almost there; he was almost at the Super Bowl. "Manning's maturity makes it a real game," read the headline from the *Free Lance-Star*. It couldn't have been more true.

All the team could do after that was wait. It was fourteen days from the win in Green Bay to the Super Bowl in Phoenix. The beginning of that time was spent resting and healing, but when the team touched down in the desert, it was all practice.

In the downtime, Eli tried to keep things in perspective. "It's not easy playing quarterback in this league in this day and age," he said to NFL.com.

"It's a learning process and you're going to make a lot of mistakes. You're going to have some bad days. It's just about forgetting those moments and learning from them. You have to put them behind you. The important thing as a quarterback is to never lose your confidence."

Finally, it was game day. Thousands of fans poured into Arizona from across the country. Eli's entire family was cheering in the stands. But Eli wanted to make sure that one person in particular was going to be there watching. It was more important to him than anything else. "Eli called me and told me that he wanted me to be there," Peyton said to ESPN. "I wouldn't miss it for the world." The two talked for a long time leading into the game. Peyton knew all about the situation—the pressure to succeed and the nervousness before the game. He just wanted to tell Eli to relax and enjoy it. He had earned it and was definitely up for the challenge. "This is obviously the biggest game that he has ever played in," Peyton said to ESPN. "It was certainly the biggest game I had ever played in last year. But I feel he is ready for the opportunity . . . I have to say that I feel strongly that this will not be the last Super Bowl that he will play in."

It was the biggest Super Bowl in almost a decade, with massive ratings and people from over 100 countries tuning in. When both teams took to the field, there was deafening cheering and fireworks. The media had turned the game into a sensation—Tom Brady and the undefeated Patriots against Eli Manning and the hard-hitting Giants—and the fans wanted a piece of the action.

The Giants won the coin toss and took the ball on the first drive. With a flash of cameras and a ball booted into the air, the biggest game of Eli's career began.

Everybody on the offense was feeling a bit jumpy, but Eli calmed them down. He reminded them that it was the same as any other game. They had almost beaten the Patriots a little less than two months before. With that pep talk, Eli settled the Giants and took the snap. It was the longest opening drive in Super Bowl history. The Patriots defense was stifling, but the Giants managed to claw their way to a field goal. Ahead of the Patriots, the Giants had a boost in confidence that carried them through the rest of the game.

It was a tough, close game. Manning couldn't find any open receivers and Jacobs couldn't seem to bash through the Patriots defense. With the clock winding down, the Patriots were ahead 14–0 in the final quarter. Tom Brady had shaken off a slow start and was back to his normal self. Eli had to respond. That's when he remembered part of the conversation he had with his brother before the big game. "You'd rather be down four points than three points," Peyton said to Eli, according to the *Times West Virginian*. Why? Because when you're down by four points in football, you have to play to win. You can't kick a field goal to tie the game and send it into overtime. You need to play your heart out. And that's just what Eli did.

With 2:39 left in the game, Eli drove his team downfield. It wasn't spectacular and it wasn't beautiful, but slowly, yard by yard, the Giants worked their way there. Giants fans were in a sweat as seconds ticked off the clock. Eli wasn't nicknamed "Easy" without reason, though. Shaking off five Patriots tacklers on one play and making a spectacular pass to a leaping David Tyree, Eli set up for the end of the drive. The touchdown was there, all he had to do was take it.

Three plays later, Eli did just that. With four wide receivers running as fast as they could, Eli hurled the ball high into the end zone and found Plaxico Burress alone. Burress caught the ball and scored the game-winning touchdown for the Giants.

Tom Brady didn't have a chance to get his own comeback special up and running. The Giants defense didn't allow him a single yard, and when they got the ball back after just four plays, Manning took the snap and kneeled down as the last few seconds of the fourth quarter ticked away.

The game was over. Eli Manning and the New York Giants had won Super Bowl XLII. In the chaos that followed, there were a thousand dramas that unfolded. Some people criticized Bill Belichick as a sore loser for leaving the field quickly, even though he had already shaken Coach Coughlin's hand and congratulated him. Others were trying to be the first to talk to Coughlin who, only a season before, was on the verge of losing his job. Hats and T-shirts reading "New York Giants: Super Bowl Champions" were being handed out.

As the excitement died down, Eli found his family. He hugged each one of them in turn. Ticker tape fluttered down, and a few minutes later—just like his brother—Eli was named Super Bowl MVP for his two touchdowns and game-winning drive.

Peyton shook his brother's hand. Both brothers had finally proven all of their critics wrong. "He showed everyone, including me, what an amazing player he was tonight," said Peyton to the *Eagle-Tribune*. "But he's always been an amazing person. I love him." Eli was overcome with emotion. For most of his life, this was what he wanted, and at that moment, he had it all. And, of course, he got to utter one of the most famous lines of all. "I'm going to Disney World," Eli said. He wasn't just going there. He was probably headed for the Hall of Fame, too.

# CHAPTER FOURTEEN
## A New York Story

An anonymous writer once said, "It couldn't have happened anywhere but in little old New York." For the Eli Manning story, it couldn't have been truer. Eli had achieved all of his dreams, despite tremendous odds against him, and he had done it in the most demanding city in the world. "I believe we play football for the greatest city in the world, and all of y'all deserve to have the greatest football team in the world," Eli said to cheering fans the day after the Super Bowl. He was a New York sports hero, just like Joe Namath, Reggie Jackson, and many other famous names.

His old mentor, Kurt Warner, put it best. "I'm excited for Eli," Warner told the *New York Daily News* after the Super Bowl. "I just remember . . . how overwhelming the situation was for him, from so many standpoints—the trade, the New York media, his brother, all the expectations put on him. You have to be excited for a guy like that. It looks like he's finally going to be able to separate himself from a lot of that other stuff. He's going to be able to create his own identity." Not only that, but Eli's accomplishments rivaled that of his brother's. Both had won Super Bowls for their cities. Both had numerous awards in high school, college, and the pros. Both had rough opening years that led to stronger second years. Both were the faces of numerous endorsements, and both helped out with different causes. Above all, both had each other to fall back on, calling once or twice a week, talking about life and occasionally football. For Eli's four years in the league and Peyton's ten, they had done a lot.

Of course, they had faced bad times as well. They had seen how a disease could change someone's life forever. They had seen how a single event could destroy an entire city. They had seen how you could accomplish a lot and still be asked to contribute more, from both fans and themselves. "I've had a lot of downs in New York," Eli said at his victory party, according to *Sports Illustrated*. "A lot of times I've thought, why have I gotten this treatment? Do I deserve this? So, to come out here and win, not just for me, but for our whole team, is really special."

But Eli had finally proven himself, not just to New York, but to everyone. He had shown the world that when a team sticks together no matter what, they can accomplish the impossible. The fact that the Giants had taken down the New England Patriots, the best team in the AFC—one of the best teams ever—was not insignificant. And it was a Manning who had done it.

Eli was on the cover of magazines, featured in newspapers, and even saw himself on bus stop ads. Thousands of people attended the Super Bowl parade in downtown Manhattan and, later, stormed into Giants Stadium for the victory rally. Eli was even asked to appear on the *Late Show With David Letterman* following the win. A standing ovation greeted Eli when he walked onstage. A year ago, the same group of people might have booed him, but now they couldn't get enough of Eli. When the cheers finally died down, David Letterman said, "You probably know, you're going to get that kind of response for the rest of your life." "I'll take it, I'll take it," said a blushing Eli Manning.

But he wasn't too big to make fun of himself. David Letterman kept giving Eli openings to bask in the warmth of the crowd, but Eli refrained each time. When they played the clip of the game-winning drive, Manning's pass twirling in the air toward the receiver, Letterman commented, "What a pretty ball that was." That was an understatement. It was the pass that won the game and it was perfect. And yet, Eli still didn't take the bait. "A spiral," he said with a wry smile. Then he continued, "That's rare for me." He was finally a Super Bowl MVP, drafted first overall, a household name, and still willing to make fun of himself. In the end, Eli wasn't so different from his brother after all.

Peyton Manning had faced all of the same sorts of trials and won the same recognition. A Super Bowl victory does a lot to silence critics. But when talking to the *Indy Star* about the next part of his career, Peyton didn't make it seem like he was just going to relax now that he had won a Super Bowl. "Whether it's realistic or not, I hope to be a better player here in this second half than I have been in the first half," Peyton said. "It will take more work physically just because of the natural wear and tear on your arm and body, but that's certainly what I'm looking for." He wasn't giving up on the Colts. He was there to stay. He was there to work and play to the top of his ability, from the kickoff until the clock ran out.

For the Manning brothers, it has been this way their entire lives. They were born into the big shadow of a former NFL quarterback and have had to earn their way into the professional ranks like anybody else. Inborn talent didn't hurt, but perseverance and playing through the pain were major factors. And neither of them are anywhere near finished with their careers. "It doesn't change my attitude, my personality, or my goals for next season," Eli said to the *New York Post*. "You still want to do it again."

And no matter what the future holds, Peyton and

Eli have each other's backs as Super Bowl winners, Super Bowl MVPs, NFL quarterbacks, brothers, and best friends.

# CHAPTER FIFTEEN
## Vital Statistics

## PEYTON'S VITAL STATS

**Born:** March 24, 1976

**Place of Birth:** New Orleans, Louisiana

**Height:** 6' 5"

**Weight:** 230 lb

**College:** University of Tennessee

**Major:** Speech Communication

**NFL Draft:** 1998, first-round pick

**Pro Bowl Selections:** 1999, 2000, 2002, 2003, 2004, 2005, 2006, 2007

**Two-time *AP* NFL MVP:** 2003, 2004

**Number:** 18, to honor his brother and father, who each wore it during their career

**College Number:** 16, which has since been retired by the University of Tennessee in honor of Peyton

**Favorite Quote:** "Pressure is something you feel only when you don't know what the hell you're doing."—Chuck Noll

**Loves:** Family

**Hates:** Losing

## ELI'S VITAL STATS

**Born:** January 3, 1981

**Place of Birth:** New Orleans, Louisiana

**Nicknames:** Easy, E-Pie

**Height:** 6' 4"

**Weight:** 225 lb

**College:** University of Mississippi (Ole Miss)

**Major:** Marketing

**College-Football Career:** Holds 47 Ole Miss game, single-season, and career records.

**NFL Draft:** 2004, first-round pick

**Favorite TV Shows:** *Seinfeld*, *Saturday Night Live*

**Favorite Foods:** Pizza, catfish, oysters

**Favorite Movies:** *Caddyshack*, *Groundhog Day*, *Major League*

**Favorite Ways to Relax:** Karaoke, work out

**Hobbies:** Golfing, hunting, antiques, gourmet wines

**College Awards:** Johnny Unitas Golden Arm Award, Southeastern Conference Player of the Year, *Associated Press* and the SEC Coaches' SEC Offensive Player of the Year, *Commercial Appeal* and the SEC Coaches' SEC Player of the Year

# CHAPTER SIXTEEN
## Peyton and Eli Online

A new season is always around the corner and the Mannings aren't done with football yet! If you want to know even more info on the Manning brothers, check out these websites online. Websites come and go, so don't worry if you can't find your favorite site, a new one is sure to pop up soon. Always be careful online and never give out any personal information while you are on the Web. And always remember to get your parent's permission before going online.

**Peyton Manning's Official site**

www.peytonmanning.com

**The Indianapolis Colts site**

www.colts.com

**Eli Manning's stats**

www.nfl.com/players/elimanning/
profile?id=MAN473170

**The New York Giants site**

www.giants.com